THE COLORFUL NORFOLK SOUTHERN

GEORGE W. HAMLIN

AMERICA
THROUGH
TIME

To the many friends, photographers and other fans that were involved in the making of the pictures in this book, and Charles W. "Wick" Moorman, visionary leader with a human understanding of the role of people and pride in the success of a large industrial organization.

Unless otherwise stated, all photos are by the author.

America Through Time®
An imprint of Sutton Publishing Inc.
www.through-time.com

First published 2025

ISBN 978-1-63499-544-3

Typeset in 10pt on 13pt Sabon
Printed and bound in England

FOREWORD

A DIGNIFIED, BUT NOT COLORFUL PAINT SCHEME

Definitely not colorful; the Norfolk Southern uses a monochromatic paint scheme, which includes only black and white, for the vast majority of its motive power, as can be seen in the photo below:

Norfolk Southern SD70 2540 looks brand-new and shiny as it heads up train 456 at South Manassas, Virginia, on October 8, 1994.

In the fall of 1989, Norfolk Southern began interchanging intermodal traffic between the Northeast and Atlanta via interchange with Conrail at Hagerstown, Maryland. Between Riverton Junction in Front Royal and Manassas (both in Virginia), these trains utilized the NS B-line, which at that time was essentially a rural branch. Conrail motive power ran through to Manassas, where it typically turned back and headed north again the same day it arrived. Pictured here is one of the early runs of NS train 235 in this service, just west of Rectortown, Virginia, on October 14, 1989.

At the formation of Conrail in 1976, the Delaware & Hudson Railway was given trackage rights to Potomac Yard in Alexandria, Virginia, to interchange with both the Southern Railway and the Richmond, Fredericksburg & Potomac Railroad at that location. Reaching northern Virginia required utilizing the Susquehanna Railroad for a portion of this journey, and that railroad's motive power often "ran through" into Southern's operating territory on NS trains 341 and 342. Here, NS 341 heads south at Bealeton, Virginia, behind NYS&W diesels including an F45 "cowl unit" on March 11, 1990.

Following the initial run-through intermodal service via Hagerstown and Manassas, as seen previously, NS and Conrail began running all of their traffic between the New York City area and the Southeastern U.S. via this routing. Conrail locomotives frequently led on the Norfolk Southern portion of the journey, as seen here on train 266, consisting of Roadrailer intermodal equipment branded as "Triple Crown" service. The northbound train is about to cross under U.S. Route 340 just south of the Virginia/West Virginia state line at Gaylord, Virginia, on May 1, 1993.

The middle locomotive seen here was a colorful and unexpected visitor on NS manifest train 456 at south Manassas, Virginia, on October 8, 1994. The red and yellow livery was for a railroad that never came to be. In the early 1980s, the Santa Fe Railway and Southern Pacific Railroad proposed to merge, but this was denied by the Interstate Commerce Commission in 1986. In the interim, the two railroads began repainting locomotives into the scheme seen here; had the merger been approved, the letters "SP" would have been placed to the left of the "SF," resulting in SPSF for the combined roads. Since this did not occur, the humorous explanation was that the four letters stood for "Shouldn't Paint So Fast."

By Halloween of 1996, Canadian Pacific had acquired Delaware & Hudson and began participating in the movement of NS trains 341 and 342, as described earlier. Thus, we see CP SD40-2 locomotive 5604 leading 341 at Bristow, Virginia; a yellow Susquehanna locomotive can be seen further back in the consist.

The next summer, on August 1, 1997, another CP locomotive in more traditional dress leads train 342 north of Shipman, Virginia.

A different member of the Canadian Pacific family, in the form of a pair of SOO Line SD60s, is seen switching NS train 12R at Marshall, Virginia, on the B-line west of Manassas on September 16, 2000.

Helm Leasing's SD45 9026 is assigned to a train of maintenance of way equipment at Glasgow, Virginia, on May 21, 2005, on the former N&W's Shenandoah line, now the NS H-line. The line to the right, protected by classic N&W color position light signals, connects with the CSX/former Chesapeake & Ohio's James River Line at nearby Balcony Falls.

By November 24, 2006, Conrail had not operated for over half a decade (divided between the NS and CSX in 1999), but many of the former CR engines retained their "dress blue" paint scheme. Leading intermodal train 228 east of Front Royal, Virginia, is a visitor from a greater distance, in the form of Union Pacific SD70M 4979.

A pair of UP units headed by SD70ACe 8582 are leading a northbound intermodal train past the crossovers at Blanchet, Kentucky, on August 9, 2013. This is on the Cincinnati–Chattanooga CNO&TP line then leased by the NS from its owner, the City of Cincinnati, on what was formally known as the Cincinnati, New Orleans & Texas Pacific. The signal bridge was known as a "boxcar" type, since the structural members had been used previously as the center sills of retired 40-foot boxcars. On the "western" double-track lines of the former Southern Railway, small single-bulb "target" signals were used in these installations, while those further east featured separate bulbs for the three colors (green, yellow, red) used to display signal indications.

This photo displays the other type of "boxcar" signal bridge, as BNSF 5705 in its "H2" paint scheme leads NS train 228 into Orange, Virginia, on January 9, 2014; in essence, we have "Big Orange" at its geographic namesake.

Canadian National Dash 9-44CW leads NS intermodal train 227 past the former N&W depot at White Post, in the northern portion of Virginia's Shenandoah Valley, on May 23, 2014. Yes, there is a white post, in the form of a highway marker, in the town; the original version was installed by George Washington during his early career as a surveyor.

Classic equipment in a classic pose with classic buildings in the background, as NS special train 045 moves Bennett Levin's privately owned E8s and passenger equipment, all painted in Pennsylvania Railroad Tuscan Red through Orange, Virginia, on May 28, 2014. This equipment was on its way to participate in the "Streamliners at Spencer" event at the North Carolina Transportation Museum. Except for the people using their cell phones for photography, this could have been the early 1960s.

A trio of Burlington Northern Santa Fe locomotives, one in the Heritage 2 scheme seen earlier, and the others in the current "Swoosh" livery lead a Norfolk Southern train west at Vermilion, Ohio, on the former New York Central's Cleveland, Ohio–Chicago line on July 4, 2014.

Just north of Lynchburg, Virginia, the former Southern Railway's Atlanta–Washington, D.C., main line crosses the James River on an impressive trestle. Leading the way on NS manifest train 12R is CEFX 1339, which belongs to CIT Rail Resources. Even more color is provided by the trailing locomotive, in the form of Santa Fe's "Warbonnet" red and silver livery in this scene on July 23, 2014.

A short while later on July 23, CEFX 1005, in a different paint scheme, leads intermodal train 212 across the James River trestle. This time the trailing unit is from the Union Pacific.

NS 12R's southbound counterpart, 11R, is seen at Milnor, Pennsylvania, on September 21 passing the then-relatively new NS intermodal facility at Greencastle on September 21, 2014, led by BNSF 7140 in the late afternoon light.

A set of Kansas City Southern SD70ACe locomotives head up NS New Jersey–Atlanta intermodal train 211, the lineal descendant of NS train 235 that we saw at the beginning of this chapter, at Marshall, Virginia, on November 21, 2014. The colorful red/yellow/black KCS livery is often referred to as the "Retro Belle" scheme, since it pays homage to the KCS's *Southern Belle* passenger train, which also used these colors.

Last light at Locust Grove (Georgia) as UP 8634 leads NS train 174 north past the traditional former Southern Railway signal, complete with metal mileage digits, on the former Southern line between Atlanta and Macon, Georgia, on June 17, 2015.

Three locomotives (and none belonging to the NS)—a pair of CSX units and a BNSF in the H2 scheme—roll empty tank car train 65X over Compton Creek, on the former N&W H-line north of Luray, Virginia, on November 23, 2015.

As noted in Chapter 1, even some of the N&W's passenger train steam locomotive liveries were more colorful than those of the early 1980s prior to the NS merger. Evidence of this is seen here, in the form of J-class number 611 forwarding its excursion consist to Manassas, south of Calverton, Virginia, on June 1, 2016.

Sometimes locomotives are themselves freight in the process of being shipped, as is the case of these General Electric products being transported to the Port of Virginia to be delivered to Colas Rail Freight in the U.K., here crossing the bridge over U.S. 29, east of Culpeper, Virginia, on April 1, 2017.

A similar international movement is taking place at Audley, Virginia, north of Berryville, as these red and black locomotives are headed for Indonesia, on June 25, 2017, as NS train 098.

The first of a large order for the Indian Railways is heading for Hampton Roads at Remington, Virginia, on August 19, 2017, again as NS 098.

NS train 228 is about to pass through Rectortown, Virginia, as it approaches the Maidstone Road grade crossing behind UP 7648, an ES44AC, and what appears to be the former BCOL (British Columbia Railway) 4610, a GE C40-8M, on November 28, 2017.

A "foreign road" heritage unit, the UP 1989, honoring the Rio Grande (Denver, Rio Grande & Western) Railroad, is seen here leading NS intermodal train 214 west out of Manassas, Virginia, on December 13, 2017.

A pair of KCS "Retro Belle" paint scheme locomotives await the completion of the switching on NS manifest train 16T so that they can take it north out of Shenandoah, Virginia, on May 3, 2018.

NS manifest train 16T, powered by colorful Kansas City Southern "Retro Belle" units is in the siding at Audley, Virginia, on May 3, 2018, to meet southbound intermodal train 203, which has a Union Pacific locomotive third in its consist.

CSX 501 leads NS intermodal train 214 into the sharp curve at Rectortown, Virginia, on the NS B-line on June 4, 2018.

Former CSX SD70MAC, now with Progress Rail reporting marks in the consist of NS 15T at Lees Crossroads, Pennsylvania, on July 18, 2018.

This pair of Canadian Pacific 4,400-horsepower AC current General Electric units lead their train of empties across the Sandusky Bay Bridge in Bay View, Ohio, August 12, 2018.

Not long after the CP-powered westbound empties, a Norfolk Southern manifest with a BNSF H1 leader and an ES44C4 (a six-axle locomotive with only four powered axles) in the current livery followed it west, with some of the roller coasters at the Cedar Point amusement park visible in the distance behind the locomotives, also on August 12, 2018.

Not all of the export locomotives moving to the Virginia Port were as colorful as the earlier examples; this set on NS train 055 seems to be in some sort of primer paint at Bristow, Virginia, on October 1, 2018.

NS premium intermodal train 27A cants to the curve just north of the Main Street Crossing in Berryville, Virginia, on December 28, 2022, with a pair of UP General Electric units for power.

BNSF 7617, an ES44DC unit, is leading train 105 (empty trash containers) north past the former N&W depot's bay window, at Boyce, Virginia, on April 24, 2023.

KCS de Mexico SD70ACe leads NS 12R north between Cody and Woods, Virginia, on April 24, 2023.

A relatively mundane NS AC44C6M leader is followed by significant coloration, in the form of UP, BNSF, and Ferromex units, as train 053 crosses the Potomac River from West Virginia to Maryland at Shepherdstown on June 15, 2023.

A "twofer," with the NS N&W heritage unit leading, and a "Swoosh" BNSF trailing as empty grain train 41T passes the former N&W depot at Boyce, Virginia, on August 1, 2023.

A good look at Union Pacific's latest version of its "Armour" Yellow/Harbormist Gray livery on the outward-facing DPU (distributed power unit) on NS manifest train 12R on May 21, 2024.

Kansas City Southern 4145 leads NS intermodal train 289 through the double reverse curves as it passes the Boyce, Virginia, depot (built by the Norfolk & Western) on May 25, 2024.

3

TENANTS

Norfolk Southern's most geographically extensive tenant is the National Railroad Passenger Corporation, better known as Amtrak. Predecessor Norfolk & Western was not required to join Amtrak at its inception, since all its remaining intercity passenger trains were discontinued when Amtrak was formed, while the Southern Railway elected to continue to operate its few remaining intercity passenger trains on its own, independently, although in cooperation with Amtrak.

In 1979, the Southern transferred the operation of its *Southern Crescent* to Amtrak, which shortened the name by removing the word "Southern." As a result, Amtrak motive power, by this time the then-ubiquitous F40PH, began making daily appearances on the Washington–New Orleans route of the *Crescent*, and this continued following the Southern-N&W merger that created today's Norfolk Southern.

Subsequently, via both organic growth at Amtrak (an example being the extension of a Northeast Regional train to Lynchburg, Virginia, and, later, via the former N&W to Roanoke) and the eventual acquisition of Conrail, which included several Amtrak routes, the NS today handles a significant number of intercity passenger trains on its routes. A hybrid example (equipment owned by the state, and operation by the NS) of this situation is the *Piedmont* service in North Carolina between Raleigh and Charlotte, which also utilizes NS trackage.

In addition to its standard livery, Amtrak also has both "heritage units" (beginning with their fortieth anniversary in 2011) as well as other "special" paint schemes. For that matter, Amtrak has gone through multiple livery changes on their locomotive fleet; currently Phase 7 is in use.

Finally, Norfolk Southern hosts a modest number of commuter operations that provide additional colorful motive power on its lines, the most prominent being the VRE (Virginia Railway Express) between Washington, D.C., and Broad Run, south of Manassas.

Amtrak's westbound *Cardinal* operates on the former Southern Railway main line between Alexandria and Orange, Virginia. This photo taken on October 21, 1990, depicts Amtrak 51 entering the double track at Calverton, Virginia, between Manassas and Orange, led by F40PH 306 in the Phase 3 Amtrak colors.

Here we have what can be considered a "sub-tenant," inasmuch as the operating authority belonged to Amtrak, which was doing so on behalf of a non-operating company, known at the time as the *American-European Express*. The AEE provided luxury rail travel utilizing streamlined passenger cars that were not acquired by Amtrak. As of March 17, 1991, at Bealeton, Virginia, it was operating on select dates over the Chicago–Washington, D.C., route of Amtrak's *Cardinal*, primarily to serve the Greenbrier resort hotel in West Virginia. Its motive power was leased, with an ex-Seaboard System B36-7 (a freight locomotive) providing the motive power, while a MARC F unit is serving as a power car for the passenger equipment.

By September 22, 1991, seen here passing the passenger station in Manassas, Virginia, the AEE had acquired its own motive power, in the form of GP40s numbers 1 and 2, both painted in the AEE's blue, cream, and yellow paint scheme, and advertising the *Greenbrier Express* service on the locomotives' noses.

In the early 1990s, Amtrak began receiving new "Genesis" P40 locomotives from General Electric. They and the later P42s would become the backbone of Amtrak's diesel motive power for many years. One of the relatively early assignments for the new equipment was the Washington, D.C.–New Orleans portion of the *Crescent*'s route. Here, P40 840 is nearing the end of its run on train 20 at Clifton, Virginia, on May 19, 1994.

The P40s were delivered in a variation of Amtrak's "Phase 3" livery, known as the "fade" scheme, which had the horizontal red, white, and blue stripes end in a pattern of dots. The 825 and 815 are passing Rapidan, Virginia, south of Culpeper, on April 1, 1995.

Now branded as the *American Orient Express*, the luxury travel purveyor was operating on the *Crescent*'s route to and from New Orleans. Motive power had become standard Amtrak F40PHs seen north of Catlett, Virginia, on August 29, 1995.

By January 13, 1996, the use of Amtrak's F40PH locomotives, dating originally from the early 1980s, was becoming less common, with the Genesis P40/42s now performing the bulk of the work. Here at South Manassas, Virginia, however, the 270 leads the northbound *Crescent* through the aftermath of a significant winter storm that had hit the Washington, D.C., region earlier in the week.

The Virginia Railway Express, formed to provide commuter train service between Washington, D.C., and Fredericksburg, as well as Manassas (the latter route using NS trackage south of Alexandria), grew rapidly in the mid- and late 1990s. As a result, the VRE leased a set of "Sounder" equipment from Sound Transport in the Pacific Northwest and utilized this equipment on both of its routes prior to delivery of additional locomotives and cars to VRE. Train 31, complete with a VRE emblem on the locomotive's nose, is arriving at the former Southern Railway passenger station in Manassas, Virginia, on September 6, 2002.

In the fall of 2009, Amtrak extended its Northeast Regional service south to Lynchburg, Virginia, on the route of the *Crescent*. Early in 2010, on January 8, train 176 is coming through Clifton, Virginia, behind P42 number 88, kicking up some of the snow on the ground in the process.

On March 7, 2011, VRE train 325, the midday westbound train on the Manassas line, is heading across the trestle at Lake Accotink Park, in Springfield, Virginia, behind relatively new MPC-36 number V52.

VRE train 329 is heading for its final destination at Broad Run, Virginia, as it departs following its station stop at Manassas on March 17, 2011. Prior to the delivery of the MPC-36 fleet, Virginia Railway Express had acquired several surplus F40PH locomotives from Amtrak; here, V36 brings up the rear, with MPC-36 unit V53 leading on the head end. The British terminology for the fore-and-aft use of motive power is known as "Top and Tail."

To celebrate its fortieth anniversary in 2011, Amtrak commissioned several "Heritage" locomotives representing the first four paint schemes utilized by the National passenger carrier on its equipment. P42 156 was chosen to represent the Phase 1 paint scheme, which featured Amtrak's "pointless arrow" logo on the side of the locomotive, and bright red on the nose. This livery was applied principally to the many EMD E units that Amtrak had prior to acquiring its own motive power. Not surprisingly, this scheme was often referred to as the "Bloody Nose"; it is seen here at Clifton, Virginia, on April 25, 2011.

On June 11, also at Clifton, the Phase 2 heritage scheme is seen applied to P42 number 66. This featured blue and red stripes of equal width, with smaller accent stripes in white. No. 66 is leading Amtrak Northeast Regional train 176.

By November 4, 2013, Amtrak's Heritage units had been joined by other "special" paint schemes, as seen here in the consist of train 20, the northbound *Crescent*, at Manassas, Virginia. F40PH 406 has been lettered to commemorate the four decades of Amtrak's existence, and ahead of it is P42 number 42 with its patriotic colors, and "America's Railroad Salutes our Veterans" slogan.

On the morning of November 4, 2013, Amtrak Northeast Regional train 176 is arriving at Manassas, Virginia, in this colorful scene that includes Ginkgo trees in their fall foliage hues, and the red of the former Southern Railway bay window caboose that is now displayed adjacent to the station.

VRE commuter train 325 heads west through the snow in Clifton, Virginia, on January 24, 2014.

This special movement, designated R051 since it is running on the route of Amtrak's *Cardinal*, is ferrying passenger cars (both Amtrak Amfleet coaches and privately-owned equipment) for use on the then-annual "New River Train" excursions in West Virginia. Here it is passing through Clifton, Virginia, on October 14, 2014, and Amtrak P42 number 42, with its slogan "America's Railroad Salutes Our Veterans," is kicking up some of the fallen leaves in the vicinity.

Here is another look at Amtrak's Phase 1 heritage unit, P42 number 156, this time pulling train 176 at Nokesville, Virginia, on February 19, 2015. From the looks of the locomotive's pilot, it appears possible that it had lived up to its "bloody nose" nickname, probably in a close encounter with wildlife.

VRE train 333 is encountering some pretty spring foliage west of Burke, Virginia, on April 24, 2015.

In addition to interstate Amtrak operations within its borders, the state of North Carolina also sponsors significant intrastate rail passenger service under the "Piedmont" brand name between Raleigh and Charlotte. Although Amtrak operates these trains, North Carolina provides the equipment. Train 73 is westbound at Concord, North Carolina, on June 17, 2015.

It is not often that you see an Amtrak electric locomotive away from the electrified territory in the northeastern U.S., but since the ACS-64 "Sprinter" locomotives were built in California, this occurred multiple times when these locomotives were being delivered. Here is number 646 behind the P42 diesel powering the eastbound *Cardinal* at Orange, Virginia, on June 24, 2015. In another 85 miles, the proverbial "new kid on the rails" will be under the electrified catenary at Washington's Union Station, and capable of proceeding on its own.

We have seen Amtrak Genesis locomotives on several occasions leading Northeast Regional train 176 through Clifton, Virginia, but this time the P42 leading the train is far from its intended service territory. Locomotive 189, decorated specifically for the *Heartland Flyer* serving Oklahoma and Texas, is promoting the "Big Game" (known as the "Red River Rivalry") between the Oklahoma and Texas college football teams.

Same location (Clifton, Virginia) a year later than the previous shot, on August 17, 2016. This time we are looking at P42 number 145 in the Phase 3 Amtrak heritage scheme, which features red, white, and blue stripes of equal widths.

Several weeks later, on September 2, 2016, Amtrak heritage unit 145 (and its reflection) is crossing Sherman's Creek at Duncannon, Pennsylvania, with the westbound *Pennsylvanian* on its way to Pittsburgh.

Back in Virginia on August 3, 2017, P42 184 is in its Phase 4 heritage livery, once again on train 176 at Clifton, Virginia.

Following the storage of P42 66, Amtrak selected P42 130 to wear the Phase 2 heritage scheme. It was also photographed at Clifton, Virginia, on train 176, this time on July 9, 2018.

North Carolina Piedmont train 78 is at Salisbury, North Carolina, on May 2, 2021 with power provided by F59PHI locomotive 1797, the *City of Asheville*.

For its fiftieth anniversary in 2021, Amtrak produced several new "special" paint schemes. This is P42 number 100 in its "Midnight Blue" livery, honoring the twenty-four-hour-a-day service provided by Amtrak employees, at Culpeper, Virginia, on June 23, 2021.

Amtrak P42 number 203 is a rolling billboard for grade crossing safety in conjunction with the "Operation Lifesaver" organization. Here, the boldly decorated locomotive is leading Northeast Regional train 176 into Manassas, Virginia, on January 13, 2022.

P42 number 160 is accelerating away from its stop in Culpeper, Virginia, on March 18, 2022, wearing the livery that debuted on Amtrak's small fleet of P32 locomotives; this design has acquired the nickname of the "Pepsi Can" (as in the beverage Pepsi-Cola) scheme.

4

NORFOLK SOUTHERN HERITAGE UNITS

In 2012, Norfolk Southern, led by its CEO Charles W. "Wick" Moorman, took to heart the suggestion of a young railroad enthusiast, and launched a program that created twenty "Heritage" units to celebrate the thirtieth anniversary of the formation of the NS. These locomotives utilized paint schemes from railroads that had been consolidated to form the modern Norfolk Southern (including the historic Norfolk Southern Railroad), Conrail and its predecessors, the Southern Railway and the Norfolk & Western.

The NS made a significant effort to ensure that the liveries chosen were accurate historically, including working with railroad enthusiast groups, historical societies, and museums to "get it right." Paint schemes from a variety of eras needed to be considered, and in some cases, the now-vanished railroads had different paint schemes for passenger and freight locomotives—the Erie Railroad being an example.

In addition, the size and shapes of today's freight locomotives are quite different from those of the postwar "streamliner" era; this also required adjustments and adaptations so that the selected designs would conform to the contours of modern locomotives.

When all twenty of the heritage units became available, Norfolk Southern arranged for a special event at the North Carolina Transportation Museum in Spencer, North Carolina (located at a former Southern Railway yard and shop facility), to celebrate. This took place on July 3 and 4 2012, and by all accounts was a resounding success, and likely will be the only time all twenty heritage units will be in the same location simultaneously.

Now that the original heritage units have been in service for over a decade, some of the fancy paint schemes have weathered considerably. Beginning in 2023, the NS has begun to repaint the heritage units, especially if they also warrant significant mechanical attention.

Enjoy this colorful group in the following pages, covering a variety of locations on the NS system.

My first NS heritage sighting (and photograph) occurred at the Railroad Museum of Pennsylvania in Strasburg on June 2, 2012. The PRR heritage unit, NS 8102, had been brought to the museum for a special event, and was on display for all to see.

In this photo taken at the event in the previous picture, an apparent paradox is visible: both the locomotive and office car to its rear are described as being "Tuscan Red," but there appear to be slightly different hues present here. In my opinion, the car's version is "redder" than that on the locomotive, which appears to me to be leaning slightly in the direction of brown. For that matter, check out the red on the PRR Keystone herald on the side of the locomotive; it is clearly a different shade of red than what is on the exterior of the 8102.

The next NS heritage unit in front of my viewfinder was the Central of Georgia representative, NS 8102. I encountered it leading manifest 37Q in Berryville, Virginia, on September 20, 2012, and chased the train south in the Shenandoah Valley. Here it is passing through the small hamlet of Rileyville—a great paint job in beautiful lighting.

NS intermodal train 227, led by the Savannah & Atlanta heritage unit, is passing South Manassas, Virgina, following a crew change at Bristow, and is heading for the junction with the B-line, which in turn will take it to H-line at Front Royal in the Shenandoah Valley. While the S&A was a component of the Central of Georgia, following the merger their locomotives were painted in the then-Southern Railway livery with "Savannah & Atlanta" titles, making this an authentic application of the heritage paint.

The paint on the New York Central heritage unit reflects the freight version of the NYC's "lightning stripe" livery, since the basic body paint is black; passenger diesels used dark gray, instead. NS 1066 is powering manifest freight 12R west on the B-line and is almost to Riverton Junction (where it will take the former N&W H-line) in Front Royal, Virginia, on September 3, 2013.

On January 9, 2014, the Wabash heritage unit is leading NS manifest train 12R north at Orange, Virginia, under one of the former Southern Railway "boxcar" signal bridges.

NS 8099 powers NS intermodal train 211 under another iconic former Southern Railway signal bridge at Bealeton, milepost 53 on the Washington–Atlanta main line on March 13, 2014.

NS 1067, the Reading heritage unit, leads empty coal train 777 north at Daniels, West Virginia, the south end of the passing siding that begins at Shenandoah Junction, on October 26, 2014. Since then, this location has experienced significant foliage growth that eliminated this view of the railroad, an unfortunate outcome from a photography perspective.

While not on railroad property owned by the Norfolk Southern, this view, on January 8, 2015, accurately depicts what is visually a Pennsylvania Railroad locomotive on what were PRR rails, at Newark, Delaware. NS manifest train W6A is waiting on track 1 for Amtrak Northeast Regional train 186, which will be making a station stop on track 2 at the Newark passenger platform. Once Amtrak's station work is completed, it will depart for Wilmington, Delaware, and head north; the freight train (operating on Amtrak trackage rights here) will follow.

Here is another look at the PRR heritage unit, as well as a friendly wave from the conductor, as NS train 12R heads west on the B-line at Thoroughfare, Virginia, west of Manassas on April 1, 2015. When the B-line began to function as a main line in the 1980s, it was un-signaled; train movements were controlled by track warrants issued by the dispatcher over the radio. As traffic built, signals were added, as can be seen here.

It looks like the CofG heritage unit, seen here on intermodal train 211 on June 24, 2015, at Orange, Virgina, has picked up some road grime in the intervening years.

The Nickel Plate heritage unit is leading empty coal train 747 west across the Susquehanna River bridge between Rockville and Marysville, Pennsylvania (north of Harrisburg), on September 6, 2015. The empties on this train are returning to the Pennsylvania coal fields from a power plant in North Carolina.

Here is a closer look at NS 8100 in its NKP garb. It features only two colors: mostly black with yellow stripes for lettering and numerals. Note the small initials just in front of the side window, the small "N.S." denoting their actual employer.

One of the smaller components making up the current Norfolk Southern was the Interstate Railroad. Contrary to the name, the railroad operated entirely within the Commonwealth of Virginia until it was acquired by the Southern Railway in 1961. At that time, it was operating a fleet of ten Alco RS-3 road switchers in the livery seen here at Lees Crossroads, Pennsylvania, on October 21, 2015. It is likely that no one associated with the pre-Southern Interstate could have imagined seeing these colors on a locomotive the size of current road diesels!

The seemingly endless string of double-stack J. B. Hunt containers on train 228 at White Post, Virginia, on February 16, 2016, certainly makes a strong visual statement, but they are easily one-upped by the classic Lackawanna Railroad (full name: Delaware, Lackawanna & Western) livery on the lead locomotive. When the Erie Railroad and the Lackawanna merged in 1960, this pleasant paint scheme was chosen for the combined company, and lasted until the Erie Lackawanna was absorbed into Conrail at its formation in 1976.

Few people now realize that today's Norfolk Southern was not the first railroad to use this name. The original Norfolk Southern operated in Virginia and North Carolina in the area between Norfolk and Charlotte until being purchased by the Southern Railway in 1974. Representing the earlier version in the heritage fleet is NS 8114, in its bright red with yellow and black accents, leading train 36Q at Mitchells, Virginia, on May 2, 2016.

Back again at Thoroughfare, Virginia, on June 12, 2016, finds the Wabash heritage unit leading manifest train 12R into Virginia's Piedmont region. The spiffy red locomotive behind it is Canadian Pacific's SD30C-ECO number 5037.

The large red "M" on the nose and sides of Monongahela heritage unit NS 8025 provide a nice color accent on the otherwise gray and white locomotive. This essentially coal-hauling railroad came into the NS system via the split of Conrail between the CSX and NS in 1999. Now, far from the namesake river valley in western Pennsylvania that the road was named for, it is forwarding ocean containers to Virginia's Atlantic Coast on train 228 at Winston, Virginia, on September 7, 2016.

Running on what was its namesake company's home rails, the N&W heritage unit is nearing Vardo Yard in Hagerstown, Maryland, with intermodal train 202 on November 10, 2016. Hagerstown was the northern extremity of the Norfolk & Western Railway, where there was considerable interchange of traffic between the N&W and the Pennsylvania and Western Maryland railroads, with the latter also forwarding traffic to and from the Reading Railroad.

The N&W in the twentieth century was not always associated with dark, dismal locomotive paint schemes. Following its lease of the Wabash Railroad in 1964, and its subsequent integration operationally, Norfolk & Western diesels began to be painted in a medium blue, dubbed "Pevler blue," so named because this hue began to appear on N&W locomotives after Herman Pevler, who came from the Wabash Railroad, became the N&W's president. After Pevler's retirement in 1970, N&W's relatively brief flirtation with colorful locomotives essentially came to an end. In the photo here, NS 8103 is leading train 228 at Cedarville, Virginia, on November 12, 2016.

Here, also on November 12, 2016, the 8103 in its Pevler Blue livery is meeting NS train 290, with SD90MAC 7333, acquired from the CIT group, in the lead. Some railfans referred to this locomotive as "Barney," the reference being a purple dinosaur in a cartoon television series having the same name.

The two types of diesels comprising the initial Norfolk Southern heritage fleet (ES44AC and SD70ACe) are large, brawny machines that tower over their antecedents. This view of the Erie unit, taken from the end of the locomotive that is not usually photographed, at Cedarville on December 22, 2016, helps to provide a visual suggestion of their powerful capabilities.

Taking a more "traditional" view of NS 1068 on the same day displays the pleasing green coloration of this unit. This is another example of the Heritage program using a livery that appeared only on passenger locomotives (in the case of the Erie, EMD E units and Alco PAs); Erie diesel freight locomotives wore black and yellow.

Black and yellow can be eye-catching, especially when the yellow is predominant. This is illustrated by the Virginian paint scheme on NS 1068 leading manifest freight 35Q at Catlett, Virginia, on January 18, 2017.

Here is another look at the Monongahela unit, again on train 228, but this time at Bristow, Virginia, which was then a crew change point just south of Manassas, on July 18, 2017.

The coloration of the Virginian unit has been likened to that of a bumblebee. Here, it is in the company of a UP locomotive featuring a different variant of yellow, on an eastbound running along the west bank of the Susquehanna River at Duncannon, Pennsylvania, on September 10, 2017.

NS 8114 leads intermodal freight 214 north on a snowy afternoon at Remington, Virginia, on March 21, 2018.

Southbound manifest freight 13R is led by the Reading unit through the Virginia Piedmont region at Rectortown on June 16, 2018.

Any lower, and the Illinois Terminal heritage unit (NS 1072) might have been effectively camouflaged by the grass, as it passes Wenger Feed's storage facilities south of Shippensburg, Pennsylvania, on July 9, 2018, on intermodal train 202.

The Conrail heritage leads NS intermodal train 20Q across Sherman's Creek at the point where it empties into the Susquehanna River at Duncannon, Pennsylvania, on May 24, 2019.

A green locomotive fitting in with the color of the verdant Virginia Piedmont countryside, as the Southern heritage unit leads OCS (Office Car Special) train 955 at Delaplane, Virginia, on September 20, 2019.

This photo shifts the color palette to orange, as NS 8015 leads intermodal train 214 in the early evening of January 25, 2020, west of Woods, Virginia, on the NS's B-line.

The Savannah & Atlanta heritage unit is on the point of intermodal train 203 at Audley, Virginia, on February 15, 2020, as it heads south on the H-Line. While not colorful, the former Southern Railway "Tuxedo" livery was certainly dignified.

The father and son playing catch next to the former N&W depot at Boyce, Virginia, have stopped to enjoy watching the Reading heritage unit lead train 13R past their location, on March 7, 2020.

Notice the non-standard modification on the Jersey Central heritage unit on train 13R awaiting a meet in the siding at Berryville, Virginia, on March 15, 2020. Hint: the googly eyes on "Miss Liberty's" silhouette were not in the official painting diagram for this unit, although they appeared on several occasions.

The meet accomplished, 13R got out of the siding at Berryville and headed south, where it is seen here at White Post, Virginia, being observed by a Clarke County sheriff's deputy, still with its "aftermarket additions" on the nose.

Now that is a lot of stripes! In addition to the trio of yellow stripes running the full length of the NKP heritage unit, there are three more on both the front and rear ends of this unit, as seen here while internodal train 203 passes through Rectortown, Virginia, on May 7, 2020.

Train 13R is holding the main line between the Woods and Cody control points, east of Front Royal, Virginia, with the Lackawanna unit leading, on June 5, 2020.

The Lehigh Valley heritage locomotive on manifest train 15T awaits an upcoming meet in Berryville, Virginia, on June 26, 2020.

OK, it does not look colorful (nor is the paint in good shape), but NS 1073 is the heritage unit honoring the Penn Central. In fact, the paint seen here is not black, but was known as "Brunswick Green," and it was applied to locomotives by the Pennsylvania Railroad. A good description of this hue was provided by a railroad modeling magazine in its directions for replicating this color: "Add one or two drops of green paint to a bottle of black." In any case, the office cars behind the 1073 do add color to this scene at Marshall, Virginia, on August 5, 2020.

Tuscan Red paint is seen here again on the PRR heritage unit as it passes through Boyce, Virginia, on August 7, 2020, with train 228 in tow. I suspect that more than a few readers would like to emulate the individual sitting in the right-hand seat in 8102's cab; what probably does not occur in that thought process is the recognition of the commitment and lengthy training required to occupy that position.

Lots of green here, due to chlorophyll for the plant life and chemistry for the paint on the lead locomotive, which some refer to as the "glow worm." Norfolk Southern train 211 at Antietam, Maryland, on August 11, 2020.

South of the previous picture's location, here is a closer view of NS 1072, representing the Illinois Terminal Railroad in the heritage fleet, on the same day as it leads 211 east of Woods, Virginia.

NS 8103 is on "home rails" here at Boyce, Virginia, since this trackage used to be the N&W's Shenandoah Line. On August 23, 2020, it is now the Norfolk Southern's H-line; the depot was built by the Norfolk & Western, however.

On the beautiful early fall afternoon of September 26, 2020, the Monongahela heritage unit leads NS intermodal train 201 past the Boyce N&W depot. By the way, this broadside view is no longer available, since a recently constructed home now blocks this view of the railroad.

The Wabash heritage unit heads up NS train 214 as it passes through Boyce, Virginia, on October 1, 2020.

Right before the sun sets, the lighting can be dramatic, as illustrated by intermodal train 228's passage through Berryville, Virginia, on October 8, 2020, with the Wabash heritage unit in the lead position.

Light engines moving south, perhaps? No, because the Reading heritage unit is displaying a marker, it is a train; in this case, NS 228, on October 27, 2020. On this day, there was no traffic between Harrisburg, Pennsylvania, and the VIP (Virginia Inland Port), north of Front Royal, Virginia, so the locomotives proceeded south to pick up the intermodal traffic waiting there, operating as a train, not light units.

"Stick Season" has arrived, at least for the deciduous trees, as the Virginian heritage unit forwards manifest train 11Z across the trestle over Compton Creek, north of Luray, Virginia, on November 13, 2020.

A few miles later, train 11Z has climbed the ruling grade southbound between Hagerstown and Shenandoah and is now "splitting the signals" (N&W color position lights) at Vaughn, Virginia, the south end of the siding that began at the appropriately titled control point at Summit, a mile-plus behind the Virginian heritage unit here.

The Penn Central unit's peeling paint is not that noticeable in this shot of NS 1073 hustling manifest train 16T north through Boyce, Virginia, on January 2, 2021. The logs to the left of the railroad here will be milled by Charles Snead's Architectural Woodwork shop located behind me, across Main Street.

A railfan videographer records NS manifest 12R as it passes through Boyce, Virginia, on January 25, 2021, with the Jersey Central heritage unit in the lead.

On February 2, 2021, the passage of NS train 201, led by the Erie heritage unit, provided a good opportunity for a snowy day "pan shot" as it passed the Boyce, Virginia, depot.

Sometimes it pays to have the camera set and ready to go even before getting out of the car, as the original Norfolk Southern heritage unit on train 228 and I arrived almost simultaneously at the Main Street grade crossing in Boyce, Virginia, on February 17, 2021.

Spring color and NS train 211 with the Erie heritage unit north of Boyce, Virginia, on April 15, 2021. Green and yellow on both the locomotive and the trackside foliage along U.S. Highway 340.

The Jersey Central heritage unit, sans googly eyes, on NS train 201 at Boyce, Virginia, on May 17, 2021.

On May 21, 2021, here is NS train 203, with the Interstate heritage unit in charge (referred to in some quarters as the "dreamsicle" paint scheme) as it nears Rectortown, Virginia.

Ready for the climb to the summit of the Blue Ridge at Linden, the original Norfolk Southern heritage unit is pulling maintenance-of-way train 92X through Markham, Virginia, on June 4, 2021.

The Blue Ridge mountains can be seen in the background as NS train 201, led by the Central of Georgia heritage unit, rolls across the Boom Road grade crossing at Audley, Virginia, on June 24, 2021.

A view of the N&W heritage unit and the N&W depot at Boyce from the other side of the tracks; NS 8103 on train 13R, July 16, 2021.

The scarecrow at the right is giving the crew in the Monongahela heritage unit on train 227 a highball indication, while the other scarecrow appears to be taking its ease, at Boyce, Virginia, on July 22, 2021.

The Jersey Central heritage unit leads manifest freight 12R across the bridge over U.S. Route 29, east of Culpeper, Virginia, on October 18, 2021.

The engineer on NS train 211 is throttling up the Savannah and Atlanta heritage unit as he brings his train into the second reverse curve at Boyce, Virginia, on May 27, 2022.

The lightning stripes on the NYC heritage unit have crossed Main Street in Boyce, Virginia, and are passing what used to be a barber shop in this small Shenandoah Valley town, as NS train 203 proceeds south on May 27, 2022.

Several weeks after the previous photo, NS 1066 returns to Clarke County, Virginia, this time at the head end of train 211, which has a significant contingent of loaded trash containers at the front of the train, on August 18, 2022.

From the Lehigh Valley in Pennsylvania to the Shenandoah Valley in Virginia, NS 8104 leads intermodal train 25A south on October 3, 2022, at Boyce, Virginia.

The Central of Georgia heritage unit NS 8101 makes another appearance in beautiful evening light on November 26, 2022, passing the station at Boyce, Virginia.

By 2023, the paint on some of the heritage units needed to be refreshed; the first to undergo this improvement was the Reading unit, seen here at Cedarville, Virginia, on train 11Z in its spiffy new garb, on April 13, 2023.

Considerably further west of its namesake, the heritage unit with the "Valley Girl" nickname is passing a set of concrete silos in rural Attica, Ohio, on August 13, 2023.

The Virginian heritage locomotive was next up for refurbishment. From the looks of it here, the cosmetic portion was a great success; view from September 14, 2023, with train 211 at the old location of Ashby, north of Front Royal, Virginia.

The Lehigh Valley unit speeds past the Boyce depot with train 25A on November 22, 2023. The house depicted in the background once belonged to the N&W, and was assigned to the maintenance foreman for this section of the railroad; more recently, it has been occupied by the former town manager of Boyce.

The green of the new crop of grass in this field at White Post, Virginia, blends in well with the same color on NS 1068, the Erie heritage unit, as train 274 heads north on March 20, 2024.

Speaking of green, here is how the Southern heritage unit looked after its makeover: great was the consensus. The 8099 is forwarding train 955 and its office cars back to Altoona, Pennsylvania, where this equipment is kept when it is not in use. Here it is crossing Virginia route 55 in The Plains, Virginia, on April 15, 2024.

Another view of the "Bumblebee," this time on train 11Z at Karo, Virginia, on the grade climbing out of the Shenandoah River valley up to Limeton on April 29, 2024.

No, it is not the early years of the NS and Conrail through trains on the Shenandoah Line; it is now the heritage unit era. The Boyce depot has been a constant during both, and here is witnessing the passage of train 13Z led by the Conrail heritage unit on May 27, 2024.

The Penn Central heritage unit looks like it should be an early candidate for refurbishment, but that does not seem to be in the immediate future, as it heads south with manifest train 13R on July 1, 2024, at Boyce, Virginia.

By July 11, 2024, the Lackawanna heritage unit has received its new coat of paint and is being recorded on video by a young railfan resident as it passes through Boyce, Virginia, with train 13R.

Here is a final look at NS 8098, the Conrail heritage unit, heading south at Berryville, Virginia, on July 26, 2024, with train 289, which includes a substantial number of trash containers at the train's head end. To the right is a relic dating back to the steam years, in the form of a classic cast-iron N&W whistle post.

5

OTHER NORFOLK SOUTHERN SPECIAL PAINT SCHEMES

Following the advent of the heritage units, the NS introduced locomotives with liveries commemorating a variety of entities. These include recognition of locomotive rebuilding/upgrading programs; industry trade groups; first responders, and their interface with the railroad; environmental factors; and recognition of NS operating employees.

NS SD60E, fresh out of the paint shop at Altoona, Pennsylvania, in its "Salutes Our Veterans" paint scheme, leads train 37Q north of Sharpsburg, Maryland, on November 9, 2012, on its way to a corporate event in Norfolk, Virginia, which was then the corporate headquarters of Norfolk Southern. The trailing locomotive in this consist was the Reading heritage unit, seen ahead of the first car in the train.

NS 6963 was painted to promote the tenth anniversary of GoRail, an organization that promotes the benefits of freight rail transportation. Like the 6920, this locomotive is also a SD60E, rebuilt from SD60 units. A feature of this series was the application of an "Admiral Cab" with its distinctive recessed cab front windows under the number boards. Here it is passing the intermediate signal at Thoroughfare, Virginia, on March 26, 2014.

NS 911, also an SD60E, was decorated in this eye-catching livery "Honoring First Responders," and it includes stickers recognizing police, fire, and emergency medical crews. It is leading local train P56 east from Manassas, at Clifton, Virginia, on June 2, 2015. This view provides a good look at the distinctive overhang of the Admiral Cab.

GP38-2 number 5642 was painted in a similar fashion to NS 911, but its slogan, "Training First Responders," reveals its purpose, "to strengthen relationships with the first responders across the NS network," according to Norfolk Southern's website. This locomotive typically is used to propel a special train of several types of freight cars used in training first responders how to deal with emergencies involving railroad equipment. Here it is operating as train 947, at Rectortown, Virginia, on June 16, 2018.

Here is a broadside look at 5642's special paint job, now at Marshall, Virginia, on June 16, 2018.

In 2015, Norfolk Southern debuted its "ECO" series of "environmentally friendly" switching locomotives for use in the Chicago and Atlanta areas. They wear an adaptation of the standard NS locomotive livery featuring two shades of green, emphasizing that they meet the Tier 3 emissions standards of the U.S. Environmental Protection Agency. On June 22, 2019, numbers 4720 (a GP33ECO) and 657 (RP-M4C Slug, an unpowered unit—note the absence of cooling fans on the roof) were working at Hapeville, Georgia.

NS locomotives 1800 and 1801 were painted in this scheme (featuring yellow paint on the cab and gray on the rest of the unit) to commemorate the conversion of SD70 units from DC electrical systems to SD70ACC locomotives with AC electrical systems. Frequently referred to as the "Butter Bonnets," the 1800 is sitting in the siding at Shenandoah Junction, West Virginia, with manifest train 16T on July 8, 2019.

NS 1801, the 1800's identical twin, is leading train 13R south at Success, Virginia, on February 21, 2020.

After the first two AC44C6M rebuilds were released in the "Blues Brothers/Blue Bonnet" scheme, several others were painted in a livery that was basically gray, with the cab and forward area in standard NS black. The 4002, seen here south of White Post, Virginia, on April 13, 2020, leading train 214, has a red "mane" behind the cab; remember, that is an NS "horsehead" next to the company's initials on the body of the locomotive.

Continuing in this series, the 4004 featured a blue mane; it is heading south at Boyce, Virginia, on April 21, 2020, with train 13R. Note the grade crossing warning device advising that a left turn here would not be a good idea while the train is passing.

"Blues Brother" number one, NS 4000, is heading north across the Compton trestle north of Luray, Virginia, with train 202 on the fine spring morning of May 1, 2020.

Here is NS 911 operating in local service on train K85 at Nokesville, Virginia, south of Manassas, on August 18, 2020. Since this is Norfolk Southern, long-hood forward operation has lots of historic precedent, although it is not seen often with wide-cab locomotives in mainline service.

Later, on August 18, the 911 is heading south at Catlett, Virginia, properly pointed cab-first.

Slug 655 and ECO unit 4717 are being forwarded north in the consist of train 214 on August 31, 2020, at Berryville, Virginia, likely for maintenance at Altoona, Pennsylvania. Note the state of Georgia emblem on the rear of the car body on both units, along with the "Working Together for a Cleaner State" slogans.

The locomotive is black, but this is a good opportunity to appreciate the Tuscan Red painted on the NS office car fleet. Train 995, a "one unit/one car wonder," is heading south at Audley, Virginia, on January 26, 2022. On its journey, it is taking the "Virginia" between Altoona, Pennsylvania, and Richmond, Virginia.

Yes, this "element" (while it obviously started life as a locomotive, and terming it a "car" would seem to be inappropriate) of the "Track Inspection and Development" consist, more commonly known as the track geometry train, is referred to as "The Brick"; it says so right on the former cab, including the quotation marks. At the time of the photo, it was parked for the night at the Front Royal wye in Virginia's Shenandoah Valley on March 21, 2022.

NS 4000, which by the way has a yellow "mane," is speeding past the former N&W depot at Boyce, Virginia, on September 14, 2023, at twilight with intermodal train 27A.

Here is the 911, "Honoring First Responders," pulling the "Training First Responders" equipment at White Post, Virginia, on May 7, 2024. It is traveling north as train NS 975.

In the summer of 2024, Norfolk Southern added a new "special paint" locomotive that is basically black with red trim. The thoroughbred is on the nose, but there is no evidence of the horsehead usually seen on the sides. The nose bears the message "Thanks To Our Railroaders," while the legend on the sides points out the critical capability of the railroad in "Moving the Weight of the World." AC44C6M 4822 is leading train 289 east of Woods, Virginia, on October 30, 2024.

Blue-nosed NS 4001 here is heading south through the Main Street grade crossing at Boyce, Virginia, on November 11, 2024, with intermodal train 27A.

A day later, on November 12, 2024, color-companion 4000 is forwarding train 27A south at nearby White Post, Virginia, as sunset nears.

6

MULTIPLE OCCURRENCES

Finally, on occasion, the colorful locomotives depicted herein run with others that fit the same description; crowds of photographers have been known to "chase" these marvelous photographic opportunities!

Here comes the Penn Central heritage unit, with its paint still intact and the "glow worm"; thank goodness NS train 21Q (retreating into the distance at the right) got out of the way when it did. Taken at Brookpark, Ohio, on June 28, 2013. The double dose of heritage units was powering crude oil unit train 65R.

The morning of June 5, 2014, brought the combination of Wabash and Southern heritage units on the front end of train 202; it is now approaching the NS intermodal facility south of Greencastle, Pennsylvania.

"Butter Bonnet" 1800 and the Savannah & Atlanta Southern Railway-style heritage unit 1065 are bringing train 12R north at Woods, Virginia, on May 10, 2020.

The same duo of "specials" as in the previous photo now have their train at Lees Crossroads in Pennsylvania's Cumberland Valley, on the way to Enola Yard on the other side of the Susquehanna River from Harrisburg, Pennsylvania.

Twelve days later, NS 1800 is now paired with another locomotive featuring quite a bit of yellow (albeit in the stripes and trim), the Nickel Plate heritage unit, south of White Post, Virginia, on the afternoon of May 22, 2020, on train 214.

The red-maned 4002 and the Southern heritage unit are pulling together on train 201 as it passes through White Post, Virginia, on June 1, 2020.

Train 12R is heading north at Boyce, Virginia, on the morning of July 10, 2020, with a pair of heritage units (the original Norfolk Southern and Norfolk & Western) leading.

Two days later, on July 12, 2020, the same heritage couplet (N&W and original NS) is now heading south at Berryville on train 228, where they are running around train 15T on the main track at this location; three special paint schemes simultaneously.

It is time for shades of blue and yellow at Boyce, Virginia, with NS 4000 and the N&W heritage heading south on train 13R on July 22, 2020.

The Nickel Plate and barely visible Lehigh Valley heritage locomotives are heading north across Old Chapel Avenue in Boyce, Virginia, on empty coal train 777 on August 2, 2020.

Further north on the same day, as train 777 crosses into Maryland from West Virginia over the Potomac River, we get a better look at the Lehigh Valley heritage unit.

On August 11, 2020, the Nickel Plate and Penn Central heritage units were teamed up on loaded coal train number 740 passing through Antietam, Maryland, and nearing the Potomac River, before crossing into West Virginia.

The Central of Georgia heritage unit looks like it has been through a lot since the photo of it in Chapter 4 taken on September 12, 2012. Now it is working together with the S&A heritage unit to get intermodal train 201 over the road at White Post, Virginia, on August 12, 2020.

The log pile is still extant as the Illinois Terminal and Monongahela heritage units roll train 202 north through Boyce, Virginia, on September 30, 2020.

On January 5, 2021, the Illinois Terminal unit is trailing "Miss Liberty," the Jersey Central heritage locomotive as they pass the former N&W depot at Boyce, Virginia.

Quite a "twofer" here as both NS locomotives that pertain to first responders are together on NS train 956, which is moving the safety training equipment south at White Post, Virginia, on November 14, 2023; red is certainly the predominant color in this shot!

NS train 955 is returning the railroad's office car fleet (plus the privately owned former New York Central "Sandy Creek" observation car, immediately behind the locomotives) to Altoona, Pennsylvania, following their annual expedition for hospitality duties at the Masters golf tournament in Georgia. The train is nearing Front Royal, Virginia, on April 15, 2024. Both heritage units assigned to this movement look great in their newly "refreshed" paint.

By late afternoon on April 15, 2024, NS train 955 is in beautiful light at Lees Crossroads, Pennsylvania. The paint on the two heritage locomotives is still gleaming, and it would not be surprising to learn that this consist had been washed prior to beginning its northward journey.

Green, yellow, red and NS black combine here on the two locomotives pulling Office Car Special 956 at Thoroughfare, Virginia, on August 22, 2024.

That is quite a message on the side of NS 4822; essentially, "Moving the Weight of the World [with] Grit, Heart [and] Drive." Railroads and railroaders operate in a unique, and often demanding, environment; the old statement about "where the rubber meets the road" pales in comparison with "where the steel wheel meets the steel rail," as train 956 heads past a corn field in White Post, Virginia, on August 22, 2024.

FINAL COMMENTS

It has been fun to look back on the photos in this book and recall some of the experiences of making them. Railroads are a truly fascinating business, and as we have seen, even some that typically project a rather conservative external appearance are not above becoming colorful on occasion. I hope that you, the reader, have enjoyed looking at these non-monochrome photos, as well as their descriptions.